ONLINE AGENCY INSIDER

"You have power over your mind – not outside events. Realize this, and you will find strength."

-Marcus Aurelius

ONLINE AGENCY
INSIDER

ULTIMATE PLAYBOOK

SIGN MORE HIGH TICKET CLIENTS FOR ONLINE MARKETING, PR, EDITING OR CONTENT AGENCY.

FRAN BEVANDA

ONLINE AGENCY
INSIDER

TABLE OF CONTENTS

DEDICATION

To my Family, for giving me the support and opportunity to chase my dreams even though they never quite understood them.

INTRODUCTION

Hi there, welcome to my world! I know you came to hear out the juice and how to start or scale a successful agency, but before we get to the juicy part, I want to introduce myself quickly so that you understand why you might want to listen to what I have to say in this book.

My name is Fran Bevanda. I'm from the small country of Croatia, located on the coast of Eastern Europe.
My last name in our native language means Water and White Wine (Bevanda= Still Water + White Wine), so you can probably guess that I've had fun meeting people and networking.

I would love to say I'm just a regular, average dude like everybody else.
But I'm not, and neither are you.

That thought is something that moved the needle for me, the realization that I was not average and I was not meant to live a normal life was the moment my life changed upside down.

That single thought, that bit of understanding, led me to where I am today.

In my 22 years, while writing this book, I built a six-figure advertising agency with more than ten people employed, and we had success spending 115 million dollars on paid traffic over three years.
Besides that, I run a few SaaS businesses, and my passion and accomplishments in the tech space are increasing daily.

But this is not an autobiography, and I know you are not here for my life story, but I will be your guide through this journey, so love it or hate it, I'm going to be the one who will take you on this rollercoaster ride of agency inner workings.

The biggest reason you should keep this book on your desk all time is the exact reason I decided to write this book.

This book is the system I spent years developing.
A system that you will have at hand to deal with all the
bottlenecks you will encounter.

So without further ado, let the journey begin.

Concept Vision Technology LLC on Cyprus,2022

WHO AM I, AND WHY SHOULD YOU LISTEN TO ME

To understand the concept behind every system and strategy I present in this book, you need to understand my background and my will to constantly seek the right path.

My story starts the same as everyone else's.
Wow, shocking!
I mean that. No successful person woke up thinking about helping any particular industry. If they told you that, they lied to you.
All of us, and you as well, woke up with two thoughts.
The first one we already addressed: "I'm not like everyone else."
The second was: "I want to be rich."

The second one will usually put you through the most pain to test whether you deserve what you asked for.

If anyone tells you they woke up one day and decided to help e-commerce brands grow, they lied.

Now with that out of the way, this is my story.

It was summer 2019, I had just finished high school, a very stressful time for every normal kid. You need to choose a college and the JOB you are willing to work for 50+ years.

Luckily, I had already started to feel that this was absurd and that I couldn't do it.

I can't work a corporate job and kiss someone's ass for 50+ years.

Still, no matter how I felt, I didn't want to disappoint my parents, so I went to college.

Once I sorted out all the paperwork (read: getting into college to make my parents proud), I still had the whole summer left.

I was always a hard working kid. I have been working in bars since I was 16, so I knew I had two months to grab some extra cash to impress the ladies when I got to college.

I got a phone call from a friend of mine. It was a job offer, a bartender on the yacht. I had to make a decision in two hours.

I had never been on a yacht, and I had no experience being a bartender on a yacht 700 kilometers from home at the age of 17. Pretty scary, huh?

I took the job, and I didn't care. I was young and full of life. What's the worst that could happen?

What I got from those two months was a lot of one-on-one experience hanging around millionaires.

If you are not familiar with how yacht charters work, people book a whole week privately on the yacht, so seven days with five to twelve people. That means we had enough time to get to know them and discuss everything.

It was summer, I was sailing on a yacht with millionaires. Salty breeze and advice on how to make millions for breakfast, lunch and dinner.

A dream come true, and it was more eye-opening than anything I had experienced in life.

But I had to work the shittiest job for 17 hours a day to hang around with millionaires. That's the price I paid.

It did two things for me.
I realized I didn't want to do bartending for even one more day.

I wanted to live like them. I wanted to take my whole family on this same trip one day.
I wanted to sail through the Croatian coast with my parents and my children, drinking some Mediterranean wine while Eros Ramazzoti plays in the background.

After I realized that, the next thing I understood was that none of them were supernatural beings.

Remember, I was 17 at the time. I thought millionaires would be the people that would talk in phrases I did not understand, do things I only saw in movies, and act like they conquered the world.

But they didn't. They didn't act in any of the ways I thought they would.
As a matter of fact, they were just ordinary people, but not average in any kind way.
They all made big moves in their lives that got them where they were.

Nine times out of ten, when I asked how they did it, the answer was: "You need to believe in yourself, kid. You need to put in the hours, and most importantly, you need to have balls."

Pretty cliche, but I memorized it.

Fran as a Yacht Bartender,2019

After the season ended in the fall of 2019, I started my college journey.

I moved in with three of my high school friends to an apartment, and we thought we would study and go to classes.
Yeah, right…

After three months of college, I only visited the building five times.

I just didn't feel it. Instead of attending classes, I spent my days thinking about those millionaires I met.
I started to spend more time investigating entrepreneurship.
This was when I first watched Robert Kiyosaki's videos where he quotes *Rich Dad, Poor Dad*.

My mind was blown! Finally, someone I share the same mindset with!

This was so new and exciting for me that I completely neglected college.

After three months and a combined five visits to my college classrooms, I decided to call my mom and tell her that I was dropping out.

I moved back into my parent's house, sat down at the table, and told my mom and dad: "I know both of you are disappointed. I want to try to accomplish something on my own. If by 30 I don't do anything with my life and none of my business ideas work out, I can always finish college in three years and find a job. I won't ask for money, I just need a roof over my head and a little bit of support."

My parents are like 40-year-old teenagers, and my relationship with them was always very friendly, in a way where I like spending time with them more than with my buddies, but during this period, my house became a cold place.

Even though my parents were supportive no matter what I decided, they still grew up very conservative.

My idea of risking my "future" to start a small business did not fit right in their heads, but they still supported me.

I had two failed business attempts in two years before I started building Concept Vision Media in 2020.

I started a construction business and a coffee shop. Both of them failed miserably.
They failed so badly that I had to leave the country to get a 9-5 so I could survive.

My parents were devastated. I left college, failed with two businesses, got into debt in my early 20s, and had no real bright light at the end of my tunnel. On top of that, I had to leave my home country so that I could get a job as an Amazon delivery driver in Germany.

Yep, you heard me right. I left my country to deliver packages for $8 an hour and I still continued chasing my dreams.

I was living in an apartment with seven other dudes who worked in construction. I didn't know a single guy, but that was another wake up call for me.

Do I want to be in my early 40s, living with strangers, working 15 hours a day for $2,000 a month, with my only joy being getting back to that smelly apartment, cracking open a few beers, lighting up a few cigarettes, and going to sleep before repeating all of it the next day?

That's not where I saw myself.

After I dealt with my companies failing, moved to another country, settled, and understood how to deliver 200 amazon packages every day, six days a week while still keeping myself sane, I started going back to what got me into the entrepreneurial space initially.

I got all the way back to understanding money, to *Rich Dad, Poor Dad*, and reprogramming my brain.

So from 6 A.M. to 6 P.M., I was delivering packages, and from 7 P.M. to 11 P.M., I was learning about business, money, and how to create wealth.

After countless research, I understood that I could start a business from home.
I could start an online business.

Even starting a brick and mortar business was complicated, and running an online business seemed much harder.

It took me approximately four months of binge watching videos, reading books, and all that good stuff to build foundational knowledge about business and money and to get broad directions on what I want to do.

You become familiar with that the first time you type "How to make money online" into Google, there is no going back.

You get flooded with ads promoting this easy beach laptop lifestyle. I became attracted to it, and I wanted to be that guy, but still, I had two failed businesses, so my skepticism levels were high, and most of those ads were something I knew worked.
I just didn't believe the guy in the ad.

As the internet has become a really loud place, and I was all alone without any idea of where to go, I decided to sit one day and write down what my perfect business needed to have on a piece of paper.

The list had the following:

- High-profit margins
- Zero to no investment
- Low risk

Those were the only three things I was concerned about. I had no money to invest. I only had time.
The coffee shop business taught me that low profit margins are a bitch.
I already had two failed businesses. It's not like I needed a third one.

Those were my guidelines for my research moving forward.

After some time, I came across a guy on YouTube talking about selling your services, selling your knowledge, and building an online service-based business that helps other businesses or customers.

All those things were entirely new to me, and the biggest point was that he addressed my three concerns in the first video.
Its high profit margins, and almost zero risk and upfront investment.

I have been hooked ever since.

My research into online business in general turned into how to sign my first client, the best outreach methods, and the best niche.

I started to understand the whole concept, the business model, and the system. The more I researched it, the more the voice in my head told me, "This is it."

Months of research turned into months of outreach, months of outreach turned into clients, and clients turned my little agency into my first successful business.

I quit Amazon after my first three clients.

After two failed businesses, three years in the trenches, from a seven roommate apartment, just an "average" Amazon delivery guy built an almost seven-figure agency.

Everything I do is anything but average.

You, the one reading this book, would not be here reading this book or showing interest in topics like this if you were average.

This introduction is just to show that it takes two non-average mindsets to conquer this book— one that will show you how to do it and another that will take it and implement it.

So let's start your non-average journey.

Delivery, 2020   Agency, 2022

SKILLS THAT YOU CAN OFFER AS A SERVICE

Let's address the true meaning of a service-based business and why more and more people have started to see the huge potential in starting an online service-based business.

Service-based business means a person who offers services to others, usually businesses.

The job of a service-based business, usually called a service provider, is to in some way help another business with their needs.

That opens a world to new opportunities.

Let's take me as an example.

I run a service-based business that helps Supplement E-commerce Brands around the world to run profitable Facebook Ads.

That's what my business does.

Service-based businesses are usually called agencies. Whoever runs an agency provides services for businesses, professionals, or customers.

Lawyers are also service-based businesses or service providers, but they don't call themselves an agency.

The easiest way to understand the difference is that it's a business that offers some kind of services and does not sell any products. They usually offer their expertise for money.

Why are service-based businesses taking the internet by storm?

When you don't have to sell any products, you don't have to invest in inventory, you have a business you can start with just knowing how to help other businesses.

As mentioned previously, it opens a whole new world of opportunities, as the prices and the products you sell are purely knowledge, help, and information you are able to provide.

Usually, prices for any given service are measured by this equation.

The bigger the problem you solve, the more you get paid.

Every industry and every company has some kind of a problem they are willing to pay money to solve. It's on you to find, address, and solve those problems.

The bigger problem you solve for richer people, the more money you will be able to charge your clients.

My all-time favorite saying is:

Solve problems for rich people. They pay more.

And you should stick to that as well.

Besides having no big investment upfront to start, you also have zero to no risk.

No upfront investment will put you in a position to avoid big risks.

Whenever you talk about starting a business, you'll always be told, "Be careful. A lot of businesses fail. It's risky."

That's what we have been taught, leading people to play it safe their whole life without making big moves.

But as we know, you are already a rebel and you have already decided to start your own business. No matter how much you are willing to risk in order to become successful, you still want to keep your sanity.

This business model is foolproof and fail-proof. No matter what happens to your business, the worst thing that can happen is that you walk away with some new skills.

I could say, "You can only lose time," but I don't look at it that way.

You will walk away with knowledge, with new experience, with much more than you came in with, and most importantly, with your first attempt at building something and standing out from the crowd.
You had the balls to try.

There's no shame in failing. But there is shame in never trying.

You tried, learned new things, and have one more experience in your book, and you didn't lose anything.

Name another business model that can give you this kind of experience. I'll wait.

Now that we have that out of the way and you know you've picked the most low-risk, high-reward path to start or scale your online business, let's address what kind of services you can offer.

The usual services people offer are:
- Paid Advertising (Google ads, Facebook ads, TikTok ads, etc.)
- Web Design
- Social Media Management (managing their social media accounts)
- Video Editing
- Programming
- CRO (Conversion Rate Optimization)
- Legal Advice
- Business Consulting
- Biohacking
- Online Education
- Online Fitness Training
- Bookkeeping Services
- PR
- Funnel Development

- Appointment Booking
- Sales Services

The list goes on and on. This business model will support whatever you can sell as a service.
 Even though people offer all of the things I mentioned above, I would still stick to services that will help rich people get more attention, and help other people become rich.

The two things I would sell as an agency owner would be attention, money or free time.
 We will talk about those in the next chapter.

To conclude this chapter, the true meaning of a service-based business is a business that sells services to other businesses, services that help that brand grow.

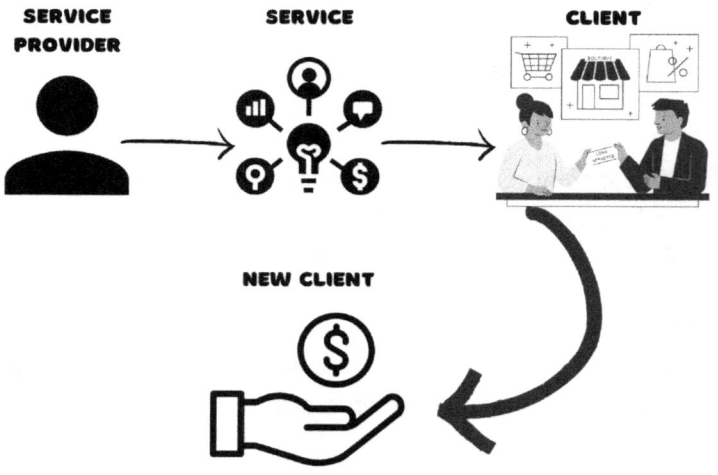

PICK THE RIGHT INDUSTRY

Now that we know what a service-based business is and what kind of skills you can offer, we need to understand what skills are the best for each growing industry.

People think that they need to be good at one of the skills I mentioned previously before offering that skill as a service to other businesses.

That's the wrong way of thinking.

Let me teach you how to think like a millionaire service-based business CEO.

Instead of first trying to understand the skills listed and then offering them to businesses you think need those services, you instead need to first find the problems that a big industry has and solve the problem.

How do you find those businesses?

Let's bring logic into this. Every business has a problem they are willing to pay X amount of money to solve.

The bigger the issue is for that business, the more they are willing to pay to solve it.
Meaning, you get paid more.

Now it's on you to find industries that pay big for solving problems.

One of my friends has a maintenance agency that fixes big airplanes.

They charge based on the situation.

If that plane needs to take off and deliver 20 tons of avocados by tomorrow, and this problem needs to be fixed today, then the price for a one hour job is $70,000.

They charge $70,000 in order to fix a one-hour problem.

What our logic tells us is that this is urgent for the company and that perhaps that single deal is worth millions and they are in a desperate situation.

If that happened and they had all the time in the world, that same service would probably be around $10,000-$20,000.

The less urgent or smaller the problem is, the less money they are willing to pay to get it solved.

Now that you know that you are looking for big problems in rich industries, let's go through some rich industries and their problems.

E-commerce - the big problem is getting more sales. If you find a brand and figure out how to increase its sales, one e-commerce client can be worth $2,000-$10,000.

Local Businesses (HVAC, Plumbing, Roofing, Solar, Fencing, Car dealerships) - all of the businesses above are well known for selling their products for a lot of money, and all of them have the same problem, finding new clients, or at least booking more appointments for their sales team. One client in this industry can be worth $10,00-$15,000.

YouTube - Believe it or not, YouTube is a whole industry, and YouTubers need one particular thing to grow and save time: video editing. If you are able to hire or edit by yourself, one YouTuber can take care of you, earning you six figures working for only one channel.

Coaching (Online Education) - Online coaches are also a part of a high paying community.
Their products are mostly at the top of the market with pricing.
For example, I joined Sam Ovens's $10,000 WeTube program with 50 other like-minded entrepreneurs.
Selling that single program and taking just 30 percent for marketing costs would get you $150,000 in revenue.

Some of the guiding principles I stick with when I choose my niche (common name for a "part of the industry") are the following:

- At least 20,000 active businesses
- High-demand market
- Knowledge and understanding of the industry

Many people think you need to meet a lot of requirements before picking the right niche.
You've probably already heard that you need to find something that interests you, something that you are passionate about, and all that nonsense.

I'm not passionate about supplements. I never was, but I'm passionate about making money, running my agency, and making other people money.

Passion is the last thing you should be thinking about when we talk about picking the right industry.

The main deciding factors should tick all the boxes.

Is there money to make in this industry? Yes.
Are there at least 20,000 active businesses so I can send my outreach without trouble? Yes.
Do I know how to solve the biggest problem in this industry? Yes.
Is there a seven-figure agency within this industry? Yes.

If you tick all the boxes, that's the niche you should go for.
No overthinking.

It's not about passion. If you like football, will you offer marketing to some low end football clubs? Of course not. They do not need your services.

What I did is I found something that will make me money in the long run and built my passion around it.

The more significant point is a deep connection with the industry.

As I already mentioned, passion is not the key, but understanding the industry at its core is.

Be intimate with the industry you pick.

What does that mean exactly?

Some of the most successful service providers are

those who worked in a particular industry, found the flaws, opened their service business, and solved those problems as a service provider.

For example, I worked ten years for a solar company, and I saw all the issues and mistakes the CEO must deal with,which is how I understood how to help him/sell him the solution.

The moral of the story, I know the ins and outs, every detail, and every possible way to position myself as a service provider to sell to this type of person.

That's the level you need to be at.
You need to be intimate with the industry you plan to serve.

Most of us will never have the opportunity to go through that process. Being employed somewhere for ten years is not a small ask, but you still have access to the internet and the opportunity to meet people online in order to understand the industry.

What I did, and what I recommend people do, is reach out to a potential client, someone I would love to work with in the industry I'm planning to start building my business in. Instead of trying to sell them something, I would tell them that I'm making something for college and that I would like to interview them.

Get this person on a 20 minute call and ask them any questions you have about them and their whole industry.

One of my favorite questions I used to ask on the calls was:

What is the biggest problem in your company right now that you would be willing to pay big money to solve?

When I asked an e-commerce supplement store owner, he replied:

I would pay $10,000 to someone who could help me sell my products on a monthly subscription basis so that I don't need to think about whether the next month will be bad and how we are going to get sales.

His response is exactly what made us successful because we found the biggest bottleneck and we turned that bottleneck into our stupidly good irresistible offer and hacked the system.

If I hadn't talked to this guy, I would still be selling something that this market does not need.

So the key indicator will not be how much you like the industry. The key indicator will be how well you understand the industry and its problems.

Once you pick a rich industry/niche with big problems that you sincerely understand and can solve, you find your perfect niche.

The most important thing is to stick to it once you find and pick one.

Every niche is hard, but the hardest one is the new one. The easiest one is the one you spend six months working on.

Switching industries will cause more harm than good.

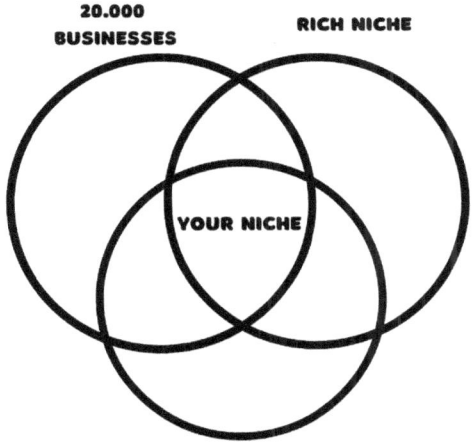

20.000 BUSINESSES

RICH NICHE

YOUR NICHE

I CAN SOLVE THE BIGGEST ISSUE
!
Ikiagi - Japanese intersection is also called the perfection or balance of life.
This is the visual Ikiagi way to present the perfect intersection in your niche Pick.

CRAFT A STUPIDLY GOOD OFFER

You can have the best service in the world.
You can solve the biggest issues possible, but if your offer sucks, you will never be able to sell your service.

The online service industry has grown by 200 percent in the last few years, resulting in many people entering the market and selling their services.

In the beginning, you could easily sell your services just by reaching out to someone and saying, ""Hey, I'll run your Facebook ads for $500. Are you down?"

Everything was fresh and new, but as we progressed, the market became more competitive, and clients started being more cautious, so even getting a reply from those business owners is an art.

So, the big question right now is how to stand out.
How can you be the one who will get a reply?

It's all about your offer.

What is an offer?

A stupidly good offer differs from your service. Trying to offer your service as an offer will just put you in the basket with everyone else sending generic messages.

Your offer is meant to sell your service.
Your service is meant to retain your clients.

In order to sell your service, you need to stick to what was mentioned at the beginning of this book.

Sell money, attention, or more time.

Meaning you will either help people to get more revenue, and more free time or you will help rich people get more attention and exposure.

Those are the only currencies businesses and professionals are interested in, that's you speaking their language.

Your service and what you do is completely irrelevant in this process.

In order to walk you through a stupidly good offer, let's talk about what a stupidly good offer is.

A stupidly good offer is an offer you can't refuse, so good that only a fool will say no to it.

Imagine someone is giving you a car for $100.
Only a fool would not buy it.
Even if you don't have $100, you'll borrow it from someone because you know this is a once in a lifetime opportunity.

That's the kind of offer we want to craft, one where people who are interested in working with us feel like we just offered them an Audi for $100, an offer they just can't leave on the table.

But dont get this phrase twisted.

Having an amazing offer is not selling your service for cheaper than market value, it's about bringing so much value that the price you charge feels like friction.

Price is what they pay, value is what they receive.

If I told you that I can make your Agency $20.000 in 3 months and that you need to pay only $5000 for the service, that is equivalent to the equation I put above.

I will make you 4x what you invested, even if you do not have the funds, you will somehow figure out the way how to get them.

I did not sell something for cheaper or charged less than market value, I increased the value you will get for paying the price we charge.

Lowering your prices as a service provider can only send your business to the grave.

How much is not enough? Do you want to have 100 clients pay you $100 a month, or do you want 1 client pay you $10,000 a month?

Here is the Offer equation built by Alex Hormozi (Source: *Alex Hormozi, $100M Offer*)

Dream Outcome ——-> Increase
Percieved Likelihood of achievement ——-> Increase
Time Delay ——-> Decrease
Effort & Sacrifice ——-> Decrease

In Alex Hormozi's book, *$100M Offer* he explained this simple example of why plastic surgeons are able to charge more for a tummy tuck/liposuction instead of gyms for the fitness boot camp.

Let's look at how long it takes a gym to get you your summer body

Dream Outcome > possible, but unlikely
Perceived likelihood of achievement> possible
Time delay> 6-12 months
Effort & Sacrifice> major

Price: $99/m

The dream outcome and perceived likelihood of achievement are unlikely as most people quit after few weeks.
It takes a lot of time to target to desired goal, and you need to put in a tremendous amount of effort in it.

Let's look at the tummy tuck

Dream Outcome > guaranteed
Perceived likelihood of achievement>guaranteed
Time delay> instant
Effort & Sacrifice> nothing

Price: $10,000

The dream outcome and perceived likelihood of achievement are guaranteed, and there is no time delay or major efforts required by the tummy tuck patients which will deliver the required and wanted outcome right away.

That is the reason why Doctors are able to sell plastic surgeries more effortlessly than gyms are able to sell their boot camps.

How we can implement that in Agency/ Online Service Providing Space?

This is the offer we created for our business:

We will add $200k to your monthly recurring revenue in 60 days without you lifting a finger, or you don't pay.

This is the offer that skyrocketed our business.

What is the true secret of this stupidly good offer?

1. **Dream Outcome** - increased, $200,000 monthly is a lot of money. It's the dream outcome for many E-Commerce brands
2. **Market Understanding** - Mentioning MRR, I showed them I understood the biggest bottleneck in their business and offered to solve it
3. **Time delay** - decreased short time delay, meaning we will deliver in 60 days, decreasing wait time for achieving the desired outcome.
4. **Perceived likelihood of achievement** -increased. They don't lose anything if we do not deliver, so the dream outcome is inevitable.
5. **Sacrifice & Effort** - decreased. They do not have to lift a finger.

Do you see anywhere where I talk about Facebook ads?
Or any kind of service?
Any kind of marketing?

I'm offering them free money.
I'm selling my service by selling money.
They pay for the money at a discount!

This offer alone gets *60-70 interested people on a call* with our sales team every single month.

Every business owner who connected with me after seeing this message told me they did not understand how we would pull this off.

The conversation gets technical once they know what we are able to do. Only then do I talk about the services and systems we use to make this possible.

None of the business owners cared about the services, and not a single person told me they didn't want to work with us because Facebook ads had not performed in the past for them.
All of them are focused on one single thing, and that's on what we are offering.

Once you craft an offer like this for your industry, appointments will start to flood your calendar.

The secret sauce of crafting one goes back to actually understanding the industry. Without that, you will not be able to position yourself and stand out.

Offers are something you can always test, change, adapt, and improve.

The offer is something I spend a lot of time working on because if you do not make your offer right, you can be the best service provider, but no one will be able to see your true potential.

If you are struggling to craft a foolproof offer, you might want to give this book a read.

Here are 8 Offers you can rewrite and use for your business:

- *We will bring you 10 appointments, or you do not pay*
- *We will bring you 15 new clients for free in 30 days*
- *We will increase your revenue by 30%, and if we don't, you don't pay a cent*
- *We will get you 10k followers for free in 60 days*
- *Let us make you one viral video for free*
- *Award-winning Agency ads management coupon, good for 60 days for free*
- *We grow your business, and you only pay us when you get paid*
- *We will add $50k to your monthly revenue in 50 days for free*

IRRESISTIBLE OFFER 101

ADDRESS THE BOTTLENECK

+

OFFER SOLUTION

+

BIG PROMISE

+

GUARANTEE

=

IRRESISTIBLE OFFER

HOW TO FIND CLIENTS

Thanks to the internet, we live in a day and age where connecting with people has never been easier.

We live in a day and age where everyone has the ability to reach out to any part of the world.
This makes this business approachable and more lucrative than ever.

Let's think about it, you can live anywhere in the world and work with someone from both the United States and the United Kingdom without physically being present in either of those countries.

My company operates in the United States and Europe, I've never seen any of my clients in person.

I have people sending me thousands and thousands of dollars without even shaking my hand in person.

This gives all online entrepreneurs the opportunity to either travel and work as they go, or to live in a more affordable country while working with clients who still get to pay less than their country's standards.

$1,000 in the US is not the same as $1,000 in Romania.

Just moving to Romania, lowering your cost of living, and charging your clients by their country's standards already gets you one step into hacking modern society, or how we love to say it lately:

Exiting the Matrix.

Even though everything is at our fingertips and connecting with people may sound easy, we need to be aware of one thing.

We are not the first ones to figure this out.

People have been reaching out and offering their services for years now, so for our offer, we need to stand out from the crowd.

In this chapter, we're going to cover everything you need to know to start reaching out properly.

- Average monthly rent in Bucharest city center: $459.35
- Average real estate price (per square foot): $226.01
- Three-course meal for 2 at mid-range restaurant: $41.47

What exactly is outreach?

Outreach is finding your potential customers and sending them your offer, the one you crafted in the previous chapter.

Let's say I see a good supplement brard on Instagram. I slide in their DMs and send them my pitch (offer). That's outreach.

We can reach out to business owners in many ways. The most popular forms of outreach are:

- Email
- Instagram DMs
- Cold Calling
- Upwork
- LinkedIn

Every niche has a different type of outreach that works best for them. If you have clients who are local businesses, it's more likely that they will respond to emails and cold calls better than to Instagram DMs, but if you're targeting e-commerce, you can't even cold call them because not a single e-commerce owner has their phone number displayed publicly.

The outreach part of getting new clients is more manual work. As mentioned previously, your pitch/offer will take care of actually getting those people interested.

We can split the outreach part into a few steps:

- Lead Sourcing
- Sending Out the Offer
- Follow-ups
- Booking the Appointment
- Free Community

Before you start sending your pitch all over the place, you need to take care of the first thing, and that's lead scraping.

Leads, commonly known as "Potential Customers," are people or information about people that represent your ideal client.

There are two types of leads
- Warm Leads
- Cold Leads

Warm Leads are people who are actively trying to find someone to help them with their marketing or who are aware of their issue.

They are aware of the problem, they are trying to solve it, and these kinds of leads are the ones that are basically waving money above their head and saying, "Take my money NOW."

As good as it sounds, those kinds of leads are hard to find. The most common places to find them are Facebook groups, Upwork or LinkedIn.

The main factor for warm leads is time, so usually, the person who acts the fastest has the best possibility of signing them as clients, so a little bit of luck plays a role here.

As we are not at Red Rock Casino and we want to have our business under our control, we like cold leads.

Cold Leads are people who are not actively trying to find someone to help them with their marketing, and they are not aware of their issue.

People you found and decided to offer your services to. It's like driving a dirty car, you might not even think about it until your car detailer says that this car could use a cleaning and gives you a good offer.
At that moment, you realize that the car is indeed dirty and that this offer is too good to not take.

We operate the same way with cold leads. When we reach out to them, we address the problem by ourselves. We are making them aware that they might have an issue that they might not even realize they have.

But not only are we telling them that they have a problem, we are also offering them the solution.

Cold leads are not interested in something straightforward because they are not trying to find help. You are there offering them your services.
So why do we love cold leads?

Whenever you have a strong offer, you have the ability to take full control of your business.

Instead of sitting in front of your PC waiting for someone to post that they need help with Facebook ads, you are taking the control and you are offering your service yourself.

We generally scrape leads in two ways:

- Do it by yourself
- Buy a list

Doing it by yourself will be more time consuming, and you are responsible for the quality.

You can create a Google Sheet, go on Instagram, and copy and paste the name of the brand and the details and you can use snov.io to detect email addresses on people's websites.

That way, you can find the email, name of the owner, and IG account for the brand.

Then you have most of what you need to reach out to the client.

But, as mentioned, it's time consuming, and if you do not have experience, it can be overwhelming.

What I suggest is buying a list from data analysts.

You can buy a list with 100 business owners for $30.

You will save yourself time and money in the end because trying to go cheaper ends with paying double the price.

First Name	Last Name	Title	Email	LinkedIn	Personal Social	Company Name	Websit
Bart	Diehl	Founder	bart@upgosupps.com	https://linkedin.com/in/ba		UpGo Supplements	upgosu
Christian	Power	Founder & F	christian@liongevitypower.com			Longevity Power	longevit
Michael	DeCarvalho	Owner-Ope	mdecarvalho@vitastrength.com	https://linkedin.com/in/m		Vitastrength	vitastre
Latricia	Wright	Founder	latricia@olive-seed.com	https://linkedin.com/in/la		Olive Seed	olive-se
Jeff	Falkoff	Co-Founder	jeff@bondimorning.com	https://www.linkedin.com		Bondi Morning	bondim
Kishore	Nannapaneni	CEO, Co-fo	kishore.nannapaneni@oralta.com	https://www.linkedin.com		Oralta	oralta.c
Doug	Blacker	Founder, CL	doug@plantrise.com	https://www.linkedin.com		Plantrise	plantris
Nahir	Luna	President	luna@organichealthlabs.com	https://www.linkedin.com		Organic Health Labs	organic
Ray	Doustdar	CEO, Foun	ray@buiced.com	https://linkedin.com/in/ra		Buiced	
Joe	Winke	Founder	joe@healthysurprise.com	https://www.linkedin.com		Healthy Surprise	healthy
Caroline	Gilbert	Co-Owner	caroline@thesmartprotein.co	https://www.linkedin.com		Smartprotein	thesma
Doug	Carlson	CEO	doug.carlson@goodidea.us	https://www.linkedin.com		Good Idea	goodide
Ted	Houlehan	President	ted@clinicallabssupplements.com	https://linkedin.com/in/te		Clinical Labs	clinicall
Erick	Quay	Founder & (	erick@dosely.com	linkedin.com/in/erickqua		Dosely	dosely.
Luiza	Reingatch	Founder	luiza@highernutrition.com	https://linkedin.com/in/lu		Higher Nutrition	highern
Rod	Stuart	Owner	rod@blenditup.com	https://linkedin.com/in/ro		Blenditup	blenditu
Noah	Alldredge	President	noah@hydrationhealth.com	https://www.linkedin.com		Hydration Health	hydratio
Gene	Lentz	President	gene@remedysnutrition.com	https://linkedin.com/in/ge		Remedy's Nutrition	remedy
Mawa	Mcqueen	Owner			https://www.livelagram.com	Mawa's Grainfreenola	grainfre
						Health & Body Nutriti	healthb
Crystal	Grant	CEO	crystalagrant@hotmail.com	https://www.linkedin.com	https://www.instagram.com	Superscript Wellness	supersc
Sandy	Kasten	Owner	skasten1@yahoo.com	https://www.linkedin.com	https://www.instagram.com	Kosher Buddha Bage	kosherl
Krystal	Vrba	Co-Founder	krystal@refreshnaturalhealth.com	https://www.linkedin.com	https://www.instagram.com	Refresh Natural Heal	refresh
Sandra	Vrba	Co-Founder	sandra@refreshnaturalhealth.com	https://linkedin.com/in/sa	https://www.instagram.com	Refresh Natural Heal	shop.re
Adriana	Florez	Founder	adriana.florez@citigroup.com	https://www.linkedin.com		Yummi Foods	yummif
Zach	Elkins	Founder	zach@leanimpactnutrition.com	https://linkedin.com/in/za		Lean Impact Nutrition	leanimp

After you have found the best approach to gather your leads, it's time to start the outreach.

Outreach is a numbers game, the more you reach out, the higher the chances of signing a client in a shorter time span.

Someone who sends 300 outreaches a day will get a client 3x faster than someone who sends 100 outreaches a day.

It's just how the outreach game works, the more volume you put in, the higher the chances of signing clients faster.

Everyone wants to sign clients ASAP, and you'd also like to close the deal now, so send 10 outreach messages and land a client.

But most of us are guilty of living in fantasy land.
I was guilty of that when I was starting out.
It's in our DNA, we just naturally want to get to the finish line first.

It's that competitive spirit in us that forces us to get everything right now, but in the business space, we need to sit down and recognize the fact that slow and steady usually wins the race.

When we understand that, we only have one option to increase the chances of signing clients faster, and that is doing 3x more work than regular agency owners or service providers.

The reason some people take ages to accomplish that is that they do not want to do it.

Everyone wants to be rich, but no one is willing to work for five years on their dream for free.

That is the society we live in today. The same people who tell you that all of this is impossible are people who were never consistent and accountable in life.

But don't hate the player, hate the game.

Now that you know that the only way to get to your goal faster is to work harder, there are a few factors you need to keep an eye on:

- Consistency
- Accountability

Consistency
You need to stay consistent with the amount of outreach you are doing. If you cheat, if you skip, you are not doing harm to any of us, it's your future is on the line, not mine.

When my future was on the line, I was sitting in my shitty, smelly room, for four days with no shower, sending emails and Instagram DMs.

I was a primal version of myself, hungry for success, and didn't care about anything else,I wouldn't sleep if I didn't send all 300 of them.

Whenever you want to "take a break," just remember that you are competing with someone like me.

Accountability
You are responsible for your wealth and your poverty. You are the only person to blame for the situation you were in, you are in, and the situation you will be in. The sooner you accept that, the sooner your life will change.

Now that you know what it takes, it's time to start sending the messages.

One of the most common pitch lines my company sends is the following:

Mark!
Love the Coco Supps story! You guys rock!
I'll be straightforward, I use a FF4R System to add an additional $200k in MRR for brands like yours, I'd like to show it to you, you wanna talk about it?

You can copy this and repurpose it for your own industry.

Most of the messages you send will not get a reply on the first message, so it's important that you stay consistent because there is a saying in the online service space:

"Money is in the follow ups."

Meaning that people respond only on their third or fourth message, so you need to be sending those people messages until they tell you either yes or tell you to fuck off.

I'm dead serious about it, my fifth or sixth message to my prospects is:

Hey Mark! Let's have a quick chat, ignoring me won't accomplish anything, I will be sending texts until you either say yes or tell me to fuck off. I'm dead serious.

So stay consistent, money is in the follow ups.

Once you get a positive reply, there is one important thing you need to know:

DO NOT SELL YOUR SERVICES OVER MESSAGES

Your goal should be to book a video call with the potential client, not to sell your service.

Do you think people feel comfortable buying something for $1,000+ from an internet stranger over Instagram DMs? That's what I thought.

The goal of the outreach messages is to sell the video meeting, not the service.

The video meeting's goal is to sell your service.

So it is important that you do not give out too much information in text messages because f you tell them too much, they will lose interest in showing up for the call.

When prospects ask me:

What's an FF4R System? is?

I respond:

Even if I tried, it would be difficult to explain it in a message. I think if we hop on a short call, everything will be much clearer, especially why it's so powerful.

Sell them a meeting and get them excited about meeting you and finding out about your strategy.

Name your strategy something unique and sexy like ours and you will get people flooding to meet with you.

When they show you interest in the appointment, send them your scheduling link.

We use Calendly, and it is more than we need.

Once you book the meeting, remind them three times before the meeting, people tend to forget and you want to avoid that.

Reminder times:

- 24 hours before the meeting
- The morning of the meeting day
- One hour before the meeting

Now that you've found prospects who have shown interest in your service/offer, it's time to jump on the call with them and sell.

Hey Fran!! Yes this week we can chat. In fact, I have free time <u>tomorrow afternoon around 4pm</u> my time. 03:15

Can we do that time on thursday
11:13 ✓✓

Or wednesday? 11:13 ✓✓

Wednesday works for me 23:52

SELL YOUR SERVICE WITHOUT THE HASSLE

Sales. You are probably sitting there and thinking to yourself, "I've never sold anything to anyone, how would I sell something that costs $1,000+?"
"I don't want to be the pushy salesman, it's not my thing."

Don't worry, I'd never sold anything in my life before I started my agency either, my only sales skill was buying Playstations for higher prices, and then whenever I got bored of them I sold them for a lower price, meaning whenever I sold something, I usually lost money.
After I learned about sales and had more than 300 sales calls, my life changed completely.
Sales are one of the most important business skills you can acquire, and as I love to say, once you learn to sell, you can never go broke.
If your whole business collapses, you can still become the best car salesman ever by using all your knowledge you've gained to make six figures.
This chapter will explain all the ins and outs of sales psychology and how you should sell your service.

SUCCESFUL CLOSED DEALS

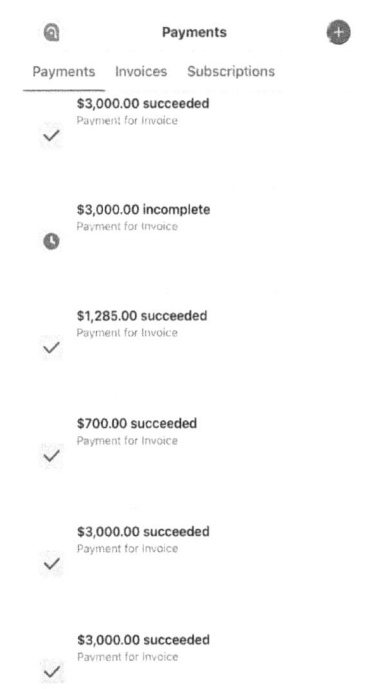

Payments

Payments   Invoices   Subscriptions

$3,000.00 succeeded
Payment for Invoice

$3,000.00 incomplete
Payment for Invoice

$1,285.00 succeeded
Payment for Invoice

$700.00 succeeded
Payment for Invoice

$3,000.00 succeeded
Payment for Invoice

$3,000.00 succeeded
Payment for Invoice

Sales are divided into a few components

- Matching the energy
- Understanding the situation
- Speaking their language
- Addressing the problem
- Emphasizing the problem
- Offering the solution
- Handling objections

When you are on sales calls, one of the most important things is the first 15 seconds.

In the first 15 seconds of the sales call, you need to match the energy the potential client is giving you.

If they are serious, you can't be goofy.
If they are goofy, you can't be serious.

People do business with people, but not any kind of people, they do business with people they like and feel might have the same way of thinking they do.
To validate this, you need to reflect or mirror the client's emotions and behavior.

You should not care if this is how you feel that day, it's important to reflect in order to attract.

At the beginning of every sales call, it's important to crack some jokes, it's important to break the ice and get the conversation started. Usually, in the beginning, I like to talk about some popular worldwide news topics, some hot topics like, "Have you seen what happened with xy?"

That way I can do one of the first steps to energy matching, I hear their opinion about some hot topic and it gives me an opportunity to agree with them , proving that we do have a similar way of thinking right from the beginning.

Whether you agree or disagree, you should always agree.

This is not a debate, you are here trying to make this prospect like you, so even if you do not agree with some of their viewpoints, agree with them and keep your own opinion to yourself.

Remember, every sales call is about the prospect, not about you.
You are irrelevant here, it's all about your prospect.
Your viewpoints, your name, and your company name don't matter.
The only things that matter are your prospect,
everything they tell you, and your offer.

They need to feel important, and your offer is here again to sell your service.
On a good sales call, the prospect talks 80 percent of the time, and you are only there to ask questions and gather information.

After you do the small talk part and match energy, the next big step is understanding and being aware of the situation and the environment

You need to ask the prospect the following questions before moving forward:

"Is there anyone you would like to join our call?"
"Do you have the next 40 minutes free?"

You make sure they will be there uninterrupted and that if they want to bring in a partner, now is the best time to do so.
You need to be sure they are in the office and that they are listening to you.

Whenever a prospect did a Zoom meeting with me from a car or on the phone while walking somewhere, that prospect never became a client.

Why? Because this is not that important to them.
That means their business had not hit rock bottom. Even though everything they are doing might be going in that direction, they still do not see this as a big problem and they are treating it that way.

Prospects who are somewhere quiet and focused on you and your service/strategy call are usually the ones ready to start today.

After you clear out and gather information about the environment, the next big step is speaking their language.

You need to use the same terminology they use. This will show that you are aware and well-versed in their industry, and it will prove that you are actually knowledgeable, and most importantly, they will feel like you understand them, and that's why they are here.

They came to this call to be understood.
Speaking their language and using terminology that is familiar in their industry will give you a free pass to their wallet.

When addressing the problem, remember you are there to ask questions, it's on them to talk.
Imagine that you are the doctor, and they are your patient.
What does a doctor do? They ask you where it hurts, what kind of pain you are experiencing, and how bad it is, and when they figure it out, they offer you medicine.

Sales works the same way. You sit down and you ask the questions, they answer, and you offer the resolution.
You offer medicine for broken businesses.
After you address the problem, you will need to turn from the doctor who wants to help the patient to a rough interrogator.

Have you ever watched a movie where they are interrogating someone, and the cop puts their finger in the suspect's wound and starts pushing in and asking for the names?

Now from being a kind doctor, you need to do exactly this. Once you find the problem, instead of offering the solution right away, you need to apply a bit more pain to it.
Why? Because you want to be sure that they understand how big of a problem this is and to make them feel like this is the end if they do not start working with you today.
You don't want them to buy tomorrow. You want them to buy today because tomorrow, the possibility of them changing their mind is 80 percent.

Once you've found the problem and applied pressure and pain, it's time to offer them the solution.

You tell them you can help, and now it's the time to talk about prices.
It's a sensitive topic.

I have a system where I always give them a price for three months for less than the monthly payments.
So I'll say, "It's $3,000 all included for three months if you do three months today, but it's $ 1,500 per month, how does that sound?"

When they tell you, "Okay, sounds good," proceed with the closing.

"Okay, cool, let's sort out the paperwork. If you don't mind, send me the company details and I'll send the invoice right away."

When you say this, they will either start doing what you said, or they will have objections.
Objections are a fun game, this is the part where you become the hard salesman.

If they tell you,

"I need to think about it."
"I need to talk to my partner."
"It's too expensive."

You need to move to barbecue conversation.
That means an open and easy going conversation with the prospect because even if you are solving one of their problems now, you have another problem down the road, a lack of trust, and maybe prices.

If you have a really strong offer, objections will rarely happen, but even if they do, it's on you to chit chat about the objections and ask more and more questions.
To give you an example, I'll run through one objection:

- I need to think about it
- Cool (always agree), for how long? Two weeks, four weeks?
- No, haha, till tomorrow, I'll give you an answer
- Oh wow, I really thought you needed to think about it, but what's gonna change tomorrow?
- I don't know. I just need time to run the numbers
- Look, I don't want to be pushy, but I'm the only one who can answer your questions. Why don't you turn off the mic and camera? I'll give you 20min, and you can run your numbers, and we can come up with an agreement.
- Yeah, you're right. Let's do this.

Objection handling is just turning lack of trust, belief, and common rejection in accepting the offer.
If the prospect does not have money, try to charge them a small setup fee just to get them onboard and give them installment payments to follow.

That's what one agency sales call looks like. It might sound overwhelming right now, but at the end of the day, sales is a skill.
The Wolf of Wall Street is the finest sales movie ever.
The 80s-90s stock market salesman is the energy you need to manifest daily.

This movie stands out because of its ferocious objection handling. They did not take the No for an answer, and neither should you.

As I said, sales is a skill. In the movie, most of the salesmen were taught how to sell, anc as the company grew, you can track the character development and how they grew from shy, stuttering salesmen to confident sales beasts.

It's about repetition, like with everything you do in life, one more rep, one more mile, one more sales call.

Each one of those will make you better and better every day.

Following the structure, not taking the no for an answer, and being aware of the sales psychology are going to make your prospects buy your products.

Sales is a skill and an art. Sales are something you should study every day and keep working on to get better. It would take 1,000 more pages to go deep down to the core of the sale, but this is on you to explore and adapt to become a beast of the salesman because all of us have it inside us, we just need to find it and reconnect with it.

CLIENT ZOOM CALL

DELIVER RESULTS AND MAKE SURE THAT THE CLIENT IS HAPPY

It's easy to sign clients, but it's hard to retain them.

Ninety percent of us who started with this business model didn't get into it to sell something for $1,000 one time to one customer.
Most of us got into it to get paid this amount every single month.
Sell a $1,000 per month service and our client will continue paying that, and from one single client, we get $12k per year basically passively.

Well, that's the dream I bought, but it does not need to be the dream you will be sold on.

What do I mean by that? When I was starting out, I thought that whenever I signed a client, they would stay.
My first client only stayed for one month.
Other clients would leave after two to three months.

I felt like my whole dream of recurring revenue was just a fantasy.

I didn't understand why the clients were leaving, I thought this whole business model was fake and that no one would pay you $1,000 a month for a year or two, no matter what everyone on the internet said.

Before you get sold on the dream that clients will stay no matter what for a long period of time, don't get fooled.

After years of running an agency with clients that are worth $50 million and more, I discovered client lifespan.

The lifetime value of Concept Vision Media clients is usually around six to nine months.

That means we have clients that work with us for two years or more and clients that leave after three months. The number we pulled is the approximate calculation.

No matter what kind of results you pull in for the clients, they will always come and go, but at least you have a clear picture of what you can expect from every client.

Even though the lifespan in our company is six to nine months, yours can be much higher, or if your service is bad, much much lower. That's why besides working on ways to increase our sales and our sales process, we focus on how to make our service even better.
It's easier to send an invoice to an old and existing client than to close a new one.

Service delivery is based on a few factors

- Communication
- Satisfaction
- Deadlines

When people invest in your service, they want to feel special.
If you are claiming that you are a high-end agency that is working with just big brands, then your customer support and service should meet their expectations.

Communication is one of the most important things in the client journey. If they feel like no one is updating them or talking with them, they will start slowly developing aversion, and that aversion will push them away from your product.
The less you communicate with them, the less connected they will be with you, meaning it will be easy for them to say goodbye after a few months.
You want to build such a strong relationship that they can't just say goodbye to you.
It's like dating a girl.
After one or two dates, you don't care, but spend six months dating her And it's not that easy to say goodbye anymore. I definitely work on communication —every single day the client gets a report and feedback from our concierge team.

Our agency has a client concierge team, meaning that the client gets one team member responsible for talking to this client and delivering all the reports they need.

Besides daily chit-chat, we do weekly Zoom video updates and bi-weekly meetings.

All of that creates a really strong connection with our clients that lasts. Once a client is signed and has paid their invoice, you, as the owner, have nothing more to do than set up a strong connection with the client.

Now you can be even more friendly and funny and can dive a bit deeper into their personal life.

I always say to my team, "I made them come.
You guys are here to make them stay, and it's again on me to make it even harder for them to leave."

As we are aware that clients come and go, and that even if we deliver the best results, they might leave, I like to play the emotional card when it comes to this, so my part of the game along their journey is to make them feel like part of the family.

For clients who stay with us for longer, we know their birthdays and we send them gifts and all the good stuff, so if they decide to switch agencies, no more chocolate truffles for birthdays from Concept Vision Media.

Now that we have the communication and experience right and they feel like they are buying a Rolls Royce of agencies, let's make sure that our results are indeed the Rolls Royce and far better than everyone else's.

If you want to operate this kind of agency, you as an owner need to be aware that without a proper media buyer or media buying team, this will not be possible, so you will need to hire the best of the best.
Some people, when I mentioned this, told me that they don't have money to employ people. The point is that all the media buyers working for Concept Vision Media are paid only when the agency gets paid.
It's called arbitrage, and I will explain it later in the book. Let's stick to the current topic.

Your media buying team's responsibility is to deliver what you promised.
I usually like to consult with them about the offers we craft to know if we can deliver what we preach.
The Media Buyer is responsible for looking over all the ads, systems, and anything related to delivering client results.

Look at it this way: your job is to sell, their part is to advertise, and while they advertise, your job is to build deep relationships with your client.
 That's the red pill of success in running an online service-based business.
If both of you do your job properly, you will have happy clients.

Treat them nicely, ask them questions, send them reports, meet the deadlines, and care.
I mean it, care about them. If you care about your clients, they will care about your agency, which is how you build a strong foundation for growth.

If you do not build a strong foundation with the first few clients, you will enter a Sisyphean Loop.

You will sign a client, and this client will leave after the first month because of the bad service and customer support, meaning if you scale to $10k/m, next month, you will be back to zero, then you will get to $10k again, and then back to zero.

That's the last thing you want to do for yourself and your agency.

Treat your clients with respect, and put your heart and soul into delivering actual results because the more vigorous the foundation you build, the more you will be able to scale.

The skyscraper has a wider and deeper foundation than a regular building, that's why a regular building stays regular, and a skyscraper is the most admired architectural work next to pyramids.

ABILITY TO GROW

STRONG FOUNDATION

HIRE THE PEOPLE AND START PUTTING THE SYSTEMS IN PLACE

Running an agency like a one-man band is something you can do for the first few clients, but that's something I would never recommend.
Running an online service-based business requires multiple tasks and each one or them needs to be executed properly.
In order to grow your business, you need people.

A common mistake a lot of beginner business owners make is trying to take care of everything themselves because they want to save money.
Instead of hiring someone, they will spend another three to four hours taking care of some unimportant task, thinking that this is the way to save and compound money.

Wrong.

Businesses need teams, they need people, name a single seven-figure business that is run by the owner without any team members.

None, there aren't any. Every million dollar business has 10+ people employed and they did not employ people because they are rich, they are rich because they employed people.

It's the same with my agency. I ran my agency with one media buyer for months.

We had around five to six clients, he was taking care of media buying and I was taking care of sales and customer support.

Don't get me wrong, this model worked fine, the only issue was that it was capped.

I had so many hours in my day, this guy had so many hours in his day and in order to grow, we needed more people with more hours.

I was always trying to save money, always scared to spend money, and that almost killed my business.

If you remember what I wrote at the beginning of the book, after two failed businesses, I was terrified to invest money back in the business.

I had around $20,000 in my bank account at that time, that was the most money I'd ever seen in my life.

I had this stupid thought that if I just reached this and if I start spending, meaning investing, i might fuck that up as well.

I lived in fear of investment until we started to lose clients.
Overnight, we lost four clients, leaving us with only two.

When your business is running okay, meaning decently, you don't have that fear or urgency to act like it's now or never.
You always feel like you have time, and as long as you have that feeling, it's hard to push and give your best.
At that moment, I was just saving, I didn't give my all, but when we lost the clients and when I felt that this might collapse, I knew I had to do something.

A wise man once said:

"In life, you will pay your price either with money or with time, it depends on what is more valuable to you"

I thought money was more valuable than time, and ended up spending six months going back and forth between six clients without being able to scale.
I had no idea or concept of how much more valuable time is than money.

Money is just energy, nothing more, fuel.

Once I started to get a deeper understanding about the whole idea of money, I started to let my guard down, and only treated money like energy instead of value.

I knew that the only way to grow was to hire more and more people.
That's what we did, we built a team.

I didn't hire a team because I'm rich.
I'm rich because I hired a team.

I know what you are thinking right now,

"Hey Fran, how am I gonna hire anyone if I don't have clients?"

"I don't have money for salaries right now."

Ladies and gentlemen, we are in the era of arbitrage, and you should use it in your agency the same way I use it in mine.

What is arbitrage?

Arbitrage is the process where you acquire something for less and sell it for more.

How does arbitrage work in the online service industry?

You first sell your service to your client for $1,000, after that, you find an expert who will deliver the service and you pay him $500, you save the difference.

That means that if the client does not pay you, you do not need to pay out the salary as every team member is hired on a per contract basis.

This is the perfect business model as, once again, it puts you in a position where you can't lose money.

Every team member I hired was familiar with this system and they were all cool with it.
Performance marketers can work on 50+ projects so your agency can be just one project along the line.

If you are paying only a low fee from one client, and there is no bright future for your agency, you can't expect people to start working for your agency full time, so your number one goal should be making sure that they deliver the results and you should not care about what side projects or main projects they are working on.

I hired all of my team members using the arbitrage model, this gave me the opportunity to actually grow as an agency while still operating almost risk free.

This opens the doors to new opportunities as you now know that even hiring team members and growing from the first client your agency signs doesn't require extra money for salaries. If you get paid, they get paid.

Later on, when you scale, you will probably introduce a new salary pricing model where some team members and employees will be hired on a fixed rate, but until then, use all the advantages of the arb trage model.

Where is the best place to find people?

- Upwork
- Facebook groups
- LinkedIn
- Agencipattern Growth Team Hubs

We used all of the sources above and the people we hired from there are still part of our team.
The key to hiring and finding the right team members is just being transparent and treating everyone nicely, and you will be good to go.
Unfortunately, I can't guarantee any platform above except the Growth Team Hubs, as they are part of our platform.
To deliver the best results, you need to have a proven track record showing that that team member was actually successful.
Faking results on the internet is easy and if you are inexperienced, you can't really judge.
Around 70 agencies that I helped told me they lost clients because of bad service delivery.

This is what caused a big problem for a lot of agency owners, and as mentioned, not a single platform is able to guarantee you quality, except ours.

We created a pool of media buyers, appointment setters, graphic designers and every position you can think of that your agency will need. We verified them all and all of them are ready to go.

One special thing we did is that everyone who is in our Growth Team Hubs Pool is willing to first work for free to prove that they are indeed the best of the best.

As mentioned, for every other platform, I can't guarantee results but with Elite and Growth Plan, you have full access to the most advanced agency recruitment pool.

The best first hires are:

- Media Buyer (after first client)
- Appointment setter (after 5 clients)
- Sales Rep (after 10 clients)

With those three team members, you can completely automate the agency and remove yourself from it, which is ultimately what you want to do.
Remove yourself, set up systems and create a cashflow business that can support your lifestyle.

Once you hire all the important roles in your agency, it's time to set up some systems.

Setting up systems for your agency will give you the opportunity to reduce the manual work and have everything working every single day.

Setting up systems is a constant puzzle of how to save time and money by removing or adding steps in work and business process.
They say that if a CEO makes one good decision in a month, they did more than everyone who worked every single day.
That's how you should think, how to improve systems, how to improve outreach, how to improve service delivery. All of those are made up of steps and processes.

For example, outreach needs its own system to work.

This is one system:

Find lead>add to sheet>send a message from 1 account>30 messages a day>10 follow-ups>0-1 meetings

This is the same system, but better and more efficient:

Buy list>5 accounts for sending messages >150 messages>70 follow-ups >5 meetings a day>1 new client

In the first step, we saved time, in the second step we saved time, increased volume, and simultaneously increased the chances of landing new clients. With this volume, we increased the amount of meetings we have every day, which ensures that with today's efforts, we can expect at least one client.

That's a good example of how a system should look. It's on you to figure out the first draft and example of your system, and to sit down and think about how you can save more time, increase volume and increase your chances of getting more clients.
That's something you should be focused on the most because this should be your job as an agency owner.

The more you play around with it, the more fun and accomplished you will feel.

Once you craft a system no one has made before, you will open another dimension to success and to your own happiness.

Only two types of systems work in this space and those are either pre-built systems or systems you build by yourself with time and experience.

Usually, the ultimate life hack is finding someone who has sick and proven systems, using their way, and through the years, improving them and making them your own. Seven-figure businesses are built on that principle alone.

INSTAGRAM
OUTREACH SYSTEM

AGENCY NUMBERS
EXPLAINED SYSTEM

SUSTAINABLE RISK
FREE BUSINESS
MODEL

FIND CLIENTS	SIGN CLIENTS	HIRE PEOPLE	GROW	OPEN A COMPANY
$0	+$5000	-$2000 +$3000	+$10,000 +$3000 =$13,000	$13,000

APPOINTEMNT BOOKING SYSTEM

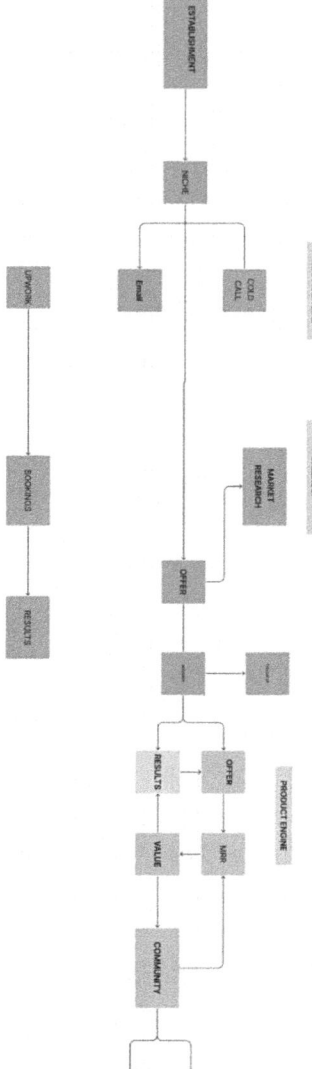

ADVANCED SYSTEM USING ALEX HORMOZIS GYMLAUNCH BUSINESS MODEL

GYM LAUNCH REMODELING FOR CVM/AGENCYLAB

MGMT + AUTHORITY + COMMUNITY

MODEL

TRAFFIC ENGINE

ESTABLISHMENT → NICHE

COLD CALL

Email

UPWORK → BOOKINGS → RESULTS

CALENDLY

MARKET RESEARCH → OFFER

PRODUCT ENGINE

OFFER

RESULTS

MRR

VALUE

COMMUNITY

MRR

UPSELLS

AGENCY SYSTEM

SMMA SYSTEM

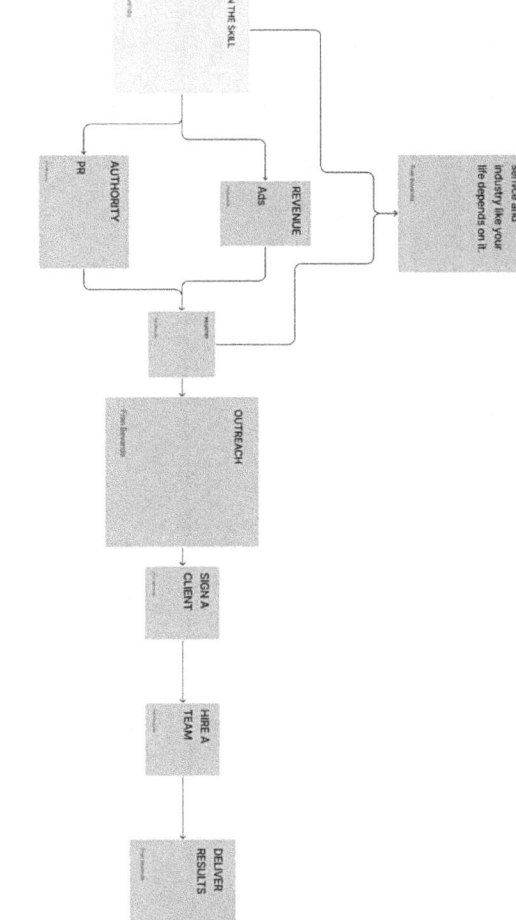

LEARN THE SKILL

BE INTIMATE
Understand your service and industry like your life depends on it.

REVENUE
Ads

AUTHORITY
PR

OUTREACH

SIGN A CLIENT

HIRE A TEAM

DELIVER RESULTS

SERVICE DELIVERY SYSTEM

BEGINNER MISTAKES AND HOW TO AVOID THEM

Even though we covered the important parts of starting and creating a six-figure online service-based business, there are still mistakes every beginner makes on their path no matter how clear some things are.
I was guilty of that as well in my beginner phase. No matter what experts say, once you actually face the demon, the reaction is way different.

I want to address the demons now, so when you encounter them along your path, you will know how to fight them.

Consider this your Failure Agency Demon's Survival Guide.

Let's begin with the most common one.

My niche is not good.

Every niche is a bitch. As soon as you understand that, you will understand that there are no perfect niches in this industry.

There is no perfect business model. Every industry is complex and difficult in the beginning.

The hardest niche is the one you start today, and the easiest one is the one that you already have six months of experience in.

Usually what happens is people start their outreach process and after 200 cold calls, emails or DMs, they do not receive a single positive reply.

This is a rare situation, but in those situations, a common feeling is that no one is interested in your service, that this niche does not need your services, that it is oversaturated, that maybe you should switch, and all that stuff.

If you get in that state of mind, that's you fighting your inner bitch.

Your inner bitch wants comfort.

No one likes to get rejected, no one likes to do work without getting results, but the question is:

For how long are you willing to sacrifice your comfort zone to succeed?

If you did every step properly, and you picked a niche that has more than 20,000 businesses, a niche that already has multiple seven-figure agencies helping that industry and you did the research into what type of service can ACTUALLY help them, you should keep your inner bitch quiet and proceed with your process.

The only time changing your niche is acceptable is when you are trying in one niche every day for 12 months and you do not sign a single client. Then changing niche and making changes is necessary.

Until then, fight your inner bitch.

I don't know anything about marketing

Most people end up thinking that their lack of experience running marketing campaigns for clients will be an issue. Because of that lack of experience, they have a hard time believing in their services, and when you do not believe in your services, you do not have the confidence to sell it to other people.

If you do not believe with your whole heart that your service is the only thing this business needs to succeed, you will have a hard time selling it to your prospects.

Confidence is built along the way, but you need to develop a deep connection with your services or media buyers so you know that you guys are able to deliver amazing results. Even though you might not be the one running the campaigns, you play the crucial role because if you do not believe in them, you will not sell them. It doesn't matter if your service is amazing or shitty, no one will ever work with you guys to find out.

Spend more time investigating your service and talking to your media buyers about it. It will help you gain a better understanding about it and build more confidence for sales calls.

Not doing enough outreach

When I say it's crucial to reach out to at least 200 people a day, I mean it's actually crucial.

Most beginners lack consistency, one day they send 200 proposals and they feel good about themselves, and tomorrow they send 50.

Don't expect much if you are inconsistent or always finding excuses why you can't do outreach.

I worked 12-hour shifts and still managed to send 200 proposals every single day.

You are battling against the players like me.

I was born on the 21st of September. On my own birthday last year, I had a two-hour sales call.
My house was full of guests, 20+ people, all of them were having fun. I was closing a client in my office.

I don't care, my purpose is bigger than 90 percent of events in my life, and even if I'm attending something, I will still find time in my schedule to do the most important tasks in my day.

Let's put it this way:

More money = more outreach

No outreach = no money

Your top priority when it comes to making money online with your agency is doing outreach.

You can neglect all the other things, leave them for tomorrow, but outreach is the only thing you cannot leave for tomorrow.

Making constant changes

If you make constant changes to your outreach every few days, you will just make it worse.

People start doing outreach, then after two days of no good responses, they try to change something.

That will get you in a loop of constant changes without knowing what you've done right or wrong.

Changes to both marketing and outreach campaigns are done every two weeks when the results are not getting better.

Remember, we are doing mass cold prospecting, so it usually takes time to pick up the pace.

Emotional connection

You need to start being comfortable with being uncomfortable.

You need to start being comfortable with people saying bad words to you.

In my career, at least 1,000 people have told me things like:

"You are pathetic"
"Fuck your agency"
"Stop harassing me you prick"
"You guys are bunch of morons"
"I wish that every marketing agency owner would just die"
"Fuck you you annoying fuck"
"This is the worst email I've ever gotten"
"Bunch of salesy amateurs!"

Do you think I care? Do you think I would let any of these words touch me?

Every year we receive 1,000+ "compliments" like these, but we also close $300,000+ revenue every single year.

When you are doing mass cold prospecting, you are reaching out to people who might not need your services, but you never know that until you actually approach them, so "compliments" like those above are common.

The worst thing people can do is get emotionally invested in every single message or bad word they get and start overthinking everything and feeling like this all person..

Its not, it's business and if you do not build a hard shell in business, you will be easily devoured by this world.

You need to become heartless and completely objective when it comes to your choices and decisions. You need to start being comfortable with being uncomfortable.

When I had hard time dealing with those bad words, I thought to myself, "Will I be able to tell my child that daddy's business did not succeed because he couldn't handle some mean words on the internet?"

I don't know about you, but that's not the story I want to tell my children.

An outreach structure that is too long

Sending long emails, DMs or Linkedin messages will not work.

Keep your outreach scripts short and simple.

When was the last time you read a long email where someone offered you something?
Exactly.

Stick with the recipe where your offer is the main character and the only question is whether the prospect would like to explore more options.

That's it, short, simple and not too complicated.
People nowadays live complicated lives, or at least they think they do. The last thing they want to read is an overcomplicated, long-ass email where someone wants to sell them something.

Not opening an actual company

It's fine to start without a company, I did that until my first $20,000 earned with my agency, but as you move forward, a company is absolutely necessary.

Most people are afraid to open the company because they are afraid of failure and because the moment they open a company, this is no longer a hobby. The real responsibilities hit and you face leaving your comfort zone.

I would recommend that you open a company immediately after your first three or four clients.

The best way to do it is to open an LLC in the U.S.A. or LTD in the UK.

It's really easy and affordable to open them and manage them.

FYI, most big companies will not transfer money to a personal account. They need real invoices to send to their bookkeepers, so when you work without an actual company, you are risking not getting paid.

Starting without a website or social media presence

Telling your clients that your website is under construction will not work.

You need a good website and social media presence that will represent you (and your company) as a true expert.

Both social media and websites can be built in under 48 hours for a few bucks.

You don't want to work hard to gain a client's trust and then lose it over not having a website.

Bad Client Relations

Once you get your first clients, you need to focus on making them feel like they bought a Porsche and not a Renault.

What I mean by that is they need to feel good throughout the process because for most of them, this will be a big move to grow their business. You need to make sure you are talking to them regularly, that you send them updates every week and that you chat with them about how satisfied they are with your services. Happy clients, successful agency.

Not building the foundations right

If you do not set up your systems and overall process from day one, your foundation will not let you grow.

I personally know a few agency owners who got ten clients in one month, but had no structure, no foundation, no real systems and they lost all their clients and had to start over from the beginning.

You don't want this to happen to you.

You want to have a system for prospecting, for sales, for onboarding and for service delivery and every team member must know what their task is when something happens.

That will allow you to bring in 20 clients at once and if everyone does their job properly, you can just grow from that point.

Not signing the agreements

Some people get so excited when someone shows interest in their service and wants to start that they do not send the agreements.

That's the worst mistake you can make.

Throughout my career, no client who did not have time or did not sign an agreement was serious.

Get the agreement signed before you do any work.

Not doing follow ups

There is a saying in the marketing world, that the money is in the follow ups.

If you are doing outreach and you send just one message to your prospects and they do not reply, you should not quit there and assume they are not interested. Instead, you should send a follow-up message.

I like to say send them messages until they either tell you to fuck off or that they are interested in speaking to you.

There was a study that showed that a normal person needs to see a $50 product at least seven times before they consider purchasing it.

Keep in mind that you are selling $1,000+ services, so follow ups are crucial.

Be realistic with your prices and offers

I know you want that $5,000 a month client right away, but it takes some time to get there.

It took me around a year before I was able to charge $24,000 for my service.

What I would suggest you do is set your pricing in such a way that you can grow with the price points.

Start with $500-$2,000 a month, find a sweet spot for your industry, and as you gain more krowledge, understanding and experience, increase your prices.

Don't lose your first clients because of greed.

Those are some of the most common mistakes that every beginner makes, read them twice to make sure you do not make them, or at least try to avoid them under any circumstances.

NO does not means NO

If you are cold calling or doing cold outreach and at every "NO" you say "Okay" and don't ask any questions, you are potentially losing thousands in client retainers.

No does not mean no, fuck off means no.

Ask questions, try to overcome their objections until they either tell you to fuck off or they hang up.

Not reinvesting in your business

Lets face it, you're getting into a business model that does not require investment and your profit margins are crazy high, so whenever you have a chance to invest back, do it.

Your focus should be on reinvesting for the first year—no trips, no celebrations, only reinvesting and building the foundation.

The best reinvestments you can make are the following:

- In-person networking and events
- More team members
- Office
- Education
- Programs
- Coaches
- Equipment (PC, mic, camera)
- Software

Avoiding innovation

Most people just become a sheep in the whole business space, you try to copy and paste success.

This kills your inner dream of being an entrepreneur.

I don't know about you, but when I was a teenager, I thought the only way to become rich was to come up with a new invention that would change the world.

This kept me in the loop of constantly innovating something new, constantly building and solving problems.

Even though I did not create a product that changed the world, my innovative way of thinking definitely changed how agencies work in the 21st century.
Don't shy away from innovation because you want to achieve the dream life faster than you deserve to achieve it.

YouTube loop

YouTube loop is when you spend most of your time binge watching YouTubers providing information.

The YouTube loop is one of the most dangerous things for every beginner entrepreneur, as it can flood your mind with shitton of new information, making you anxious and overwhelmed, leaving you not knowing how to start.

When I started my agency, I had an anxiety attack because of the YouTube loop.

I started to feel like every YouTuber was messing with my head and that there was no real solution to actually starting an agency. I started to feel short of breath and I had to go for a quick walk.

I just felt like I needed to get out, out, out.

I started to walk, no cell phone, nothing, just me and my thoughts.
After some deep breaths, I started solving the problem by myself and I came to a realization.

The biggest problem I had was listening to six YouTubers, with six different approaches and six different strategies.

There were six different opinions and the only thing I wanted was one solution.

The only way to solve that was to find someone I liked the most, someone I connected with the most, someone I trust.

Then I reached out and asked if there was a way they could coach me and help me on the way.

At that time, that was the biggest and scariest investment for me.

It turned out to be the best decision I ever made.

Silencing every other voice and only listening to one guy who wanted to help me whole-heartedly got me to $5k/month in less than two months.

The YouTube loop will be a problem for ignorant individuals unwilling to invest in proper guidance and education, but if you are a smart person, you will find a true, pure-hearted person to help you on your path.

We can't do everything alone, each one of us needs help.

Lack of focus

We all live in a busy and loud world where focus, meaning true, actual focus, is more valuable than gold.

Human beings who are able to maintain deep focus and innovate are the ones that are on the front pages of Forbes.

You are probably reading this book, ready to finish it and to start building your business, but five days ago your screen time on your phone was probably three to four hours a day.

Social media and your phone can be real enemies while building your business, as so much content is available nowadays to suck us into an infinite loop of nothingness.

Try this trickL let someone who either lives with you or hangs around with you start scrolling through TikTok. After 15 minutes of scrolling, take their phone away and ask them what happened in the last four videos they watched.

They will not have a clue.

Once you understand that playing with your dog for four hours a day is more valuable and leaves you more memories, you understand how toxic this content is.

My good friend David said that every social media user is either a buyer or a seller.

Your goal is to be the seller, to understand the algorithm and instead of turning yourself into focus-less zombie, turn yourself into a business owner who leveraged the influence of the algorithm to build wealth.

Avoiding Help

This business is saturated and ruthless, and one of the curses and blessings is that most of the information is out there.

As I mentioned in the YouTube loop, a lot of new agency owners get flooded with information and they refuse to invest in proper help and education.

The best way to save time, money and nerves is investing in a proper program or mentor who will personally help you along the way.

Crafting Mediocre Offers

Most people understand that the offer is really important, a vehicle for your business, but then craft a mediocre offer with a lousy guarantee and they think that's it.

To craft an amazing offer, you need to spend weeks analyzing your market needs and how you're going to approach prospects with a system and offer they would feel stupid saying no to.

Don't rush this process because if you send mediocre and lousy offers, every other effort is worthless.

Sending outreach messages that are too long

Keep the small talk to a minimum and be direct with everything you have to say.

People appreciate you being direct and not wasting their time pretending you care where they are from.

Your offer should be so penetrating that you can use your first message as an entry point.

Play the volume and speed game, not the fake personalization garbage game.

FINAL WORD

We've explained what an agency actually is, what service based businesses are all about, how to craft your offer, how to find your industry, and how to deliver the best results to keep both your clients and yourself happy.
We covered every detail needed to start the right way and understand all the core values of this business model.

I would like to say that this book was written for 17-year-old me.

A young individual trying to figure out life.

This is the tone I wrote this book in, no fancy or complicated words, plain execution and understanding. I like to say that people who can't explain what they do to a child do not understand how to do it themselves either.

I tried to make this book as readable as possible, the end goal is not for you to admire the book and the words I put in it, but instead use it as a guide through your online business journey, signing your first client and sending me a text to let me know that my book helped you.

That's what we want to accomplish with the book: open doors to the online business space to all young entrepreneurs who are lost in this loud space in the era of social media.

Besides executing things using the model from the book, there are few things that I want to mention that I struggled with while starting my agency.

Self-doubt and FOMO

Those two combined happen to every young entrepreneur, the weak ones did not resist it and they gave up.
Self-doubt and FOMO come as a package when you start focusing on yourself and your future.

You are about to do something that society told you that you can't do.

In their eyes, it is equivalent of saying you are planning to jump from the building and land on your feet like nothing happened. That is how they see you and your little business.

No matter what they think, you are still about to do it and self-doubt is normal.

You can't avoid it, you are starting in a direction everyone is telling you not to go, you are exiting the comfort zone with every step forward you take.

Why am I mentioning this? I need you to understand that it's perfectly okay to feel self-doubt, you just don't have to listen to it.

Be strong and do not overthink what if it fails? What if it doesn't fail?"

Besides self-doubt, the entrepreneurial path is lonely in the beginning, you are far from popping bottles and fancy dinners. Before you get anywhere near that, you need to go through years of suffering, isolation and dedication.

Sounds bad? It should sound bad.

The worse it sounds, the better your story will be one day.

One of the greatest speakers for me personally, Jordan B Peterson, said that men should be monsters, capable of everything.

As a man of dedication, suffering and honor, I felt that. The goal is not to have an easy path to win, the goal is to have it as hard as possible. Building businesses is next to sport and the armed forces as the biggest character building activity.

If you gave me $100,000 a few years ago, I would have spent it on stupid things. I never earned that money, I never understood money, I've never been in a dark place for long enough to deserve that money, so whenever you hear someone say that if you give money to a broke man, he will be broke again tomorrow, it is absolutely true.

It's not about money, it's about the character you build and the person you become with the money you make.

The Fran who made $2k per month is not the Fran that makes $50k per month, it's a lvl 1 character and a lvl 20 character we are talking about and both of them are built in a dark, isolated place nurtured with FOMO.

Fear Of Missing Out or FOMO is the feeling that develops when you see everyone having a good time, good life and you start getting anxious that you are missing out on life.

Once you understand that you are missing out on life and you want to make a change, life will put you in an even darker and even more isolated place because you will start to understand some things. You will understand how life works.

In those moments, life will feel really dark, but you will know you are on the right path.

It's okay to feel, but it's not okay to listen your feelings. Do not listen to them.
Your brain wants comfort, do not give it.

You feel tired? Stick to your schedule.
You feel sick? Stick to your schedule.
You wanna go out? Stick to your schedule.
You feel depressed? Stick to your schedule.
You feel anxious? Stick to your schedule.
Your girlfriend/boyfriend left? Stick to your schedule.

Your ability to stick to your purpose and goals no matter the circumstances is where the true leaders are born. When the rest of the society stops, and you keep pushing forward is where the true one percent are born.

It's player vs. player, and you are competing with someone like me.
The way I feel does not affect what I'm going to do that day, I'll wake up and work my ass off, then go to sleep. I do not care.

My purpose in life is more important to me than one potentially exhausting day.

Your success will be measured with the amount of stress and shit you can take.

No one says it's gonna be easy, it is stupidly simple, but it aint gonna be easy.

You have one of the greatest opportunities in your life in front of you right now, don't waste it because of one headache and sore legs.

This book should be your guide to start and execute as you go. Besides the book, we also have an educational platform we built for agency owners and online service providers.

The platform is called Agencipattern, and you can find it at agencipattern.co.

It's the first ever platform and mobile app for SMMA, agency owners and online service providers that is super affordable to anyone and has a 100 percent full money back guarantee.

You heard me right, we will either help you or you'll get your money back.

All that, plus we are the most affordable on the market, and we plan to maintain that position.

I like to say that I built this for young Fran, who is just starting out,the Fran who did not believe in programs.

The first program I invested in was cheap, but had no guarantee and no actual information.

Instead of a program, we built a whole educational company, we made it affordable, and we believe in ourselves so much that we offer a full money back guarantee.

We helped more than 300 agencies start successfully and scale with my personal guidance.
We made adding five new clients every month standard for the agencies we work with.

I'm not here to brag about how cool we are and how well we are able to scale agencies. Instead, I'm here to say thank you.

As a current or future agency owner, you took your time to read something I wrote.

To you it might be just a cool book with some good information, but for me this was a long project that took months and months to write, and for someone who never did well in school, writing a book was a big step for me.

But writing is one part, having someone to read it from start to finish brings warmth and I can't thank you enough.

As a thank you, I want to give you something back as well.

You can use the code **AGENCIEMPIRE10** for 10 percent off on Growth and Elite Plans on our platform.

I don't want to pitch you anything, or sell you something. I just want to mention that if you are considering joining a community of agency owners who are growing day by day with each other,if you are looking for a community that will help you and you don't want to build in silence anymore without any guidance and not knowing is your next move the right move or not having someone to help you to make the right decision, we've built something that takes care of exactly that.

Beside that, we also have one yearly trip for the best members, and this could easily be you.

Scan the QR code to find out more about this

And, for the individuals that are looking for **Growth Partner** for their agency, we will come in your Agency to personally help you 1 on 1 to build out your whole client acquisition system, sales system and team management system using our **Cold Blooded Acquisition** apporach without you lifting a finger.

Scan the QR code to find out more about this

If you are ready to crush it with us, now is your chance.

Even if you don't, I'm happy to see you here on the last pages of my book.

If I opened your eyes, shared a good tip, gave you a different perspective, shifted your mindset, or anything through my words, then my mission was accomplished.

Thank you for having me, good luck my friend, and I hope we cross paths again in the future!

Love,
Fran

SOME AGENCIPATTERN RESULTS

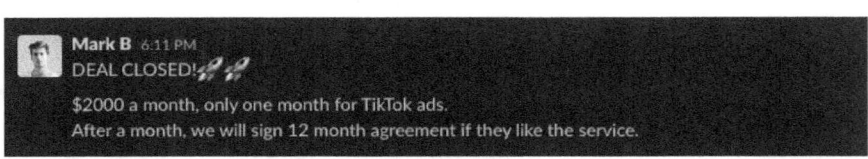

Mark B 6:11 PM
DEAL CLOSED!
$2000 a month, only one month for TikTok ads.
After a month, we will sign 12 month agreement if they like the service.

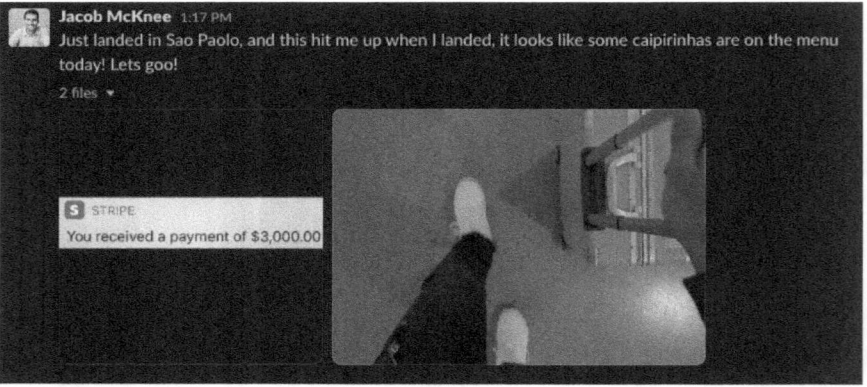

Jacob McKnee 1:17 PM
Just landed in Sao Paolo, and this hit me up when I landed, it looks like some caipirinhas are on the menu today! Lets goo!
2 files ▾

S STRIPE
You received a payment of $3,000.00

Aurelius Z 6:49 PM
$27,500 collected this month.
Goal was $10k, looks like we exceeded it a bit hahhaha

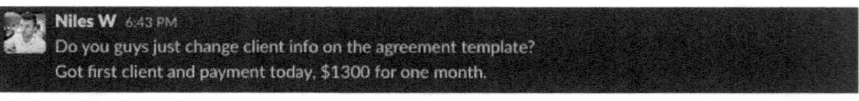

Niles W 6:43 PM
Do you guys just change client info on the agreement template?
Got first client and payment today, $1300 for one month.

Wolfgang P 6:47 PM
I know everyone was against of me changing the niche
but 2 weeks in new niche Fran recommended me, 10 meetings booked and 2 clients closed
looks like it works!

Luca F 6:35 PM
From $3k/m to $8k/m in 2 months.

Best investment fr

We closed another recruitment agency today

Mark J.
Another one today but the fifth this month! Small $1,500 retainer, e-com! Guys, This is changing my life for real

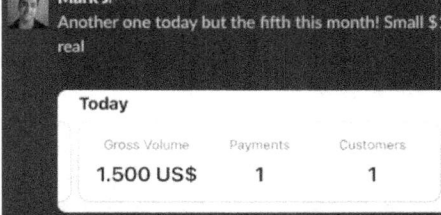

Today

Gross Volume	Payments	Customers
1.500 US$	1	1

Roman V 6:21 PM
We hit $5k in 10 days of the new month, aiming to finish as our first $10k month.
Looks like Fran was right it was just a single tweak in the offer to make it work.

Anthony P 6:14 PM
I just got off the meeting with $100k/m Ecom Brand.
The second closing meeting is locked.
Number collected and will be sending them business manager overview today.

David H

Bro, I can't believe that this is happening. I mean I have been researching a lot about all of this, but you remember when we chatted, I told you that I'm clueless about running businesses and especially any kind of marketing at all. I will never forget that you didn't ask me anything except one question "Do you have the will and balls to go for it?" 2 months later, my stripe is looking like this. I don't want to go ahead of myself, I know I need to grind now even more, but at least now I know what I'm grinding for.

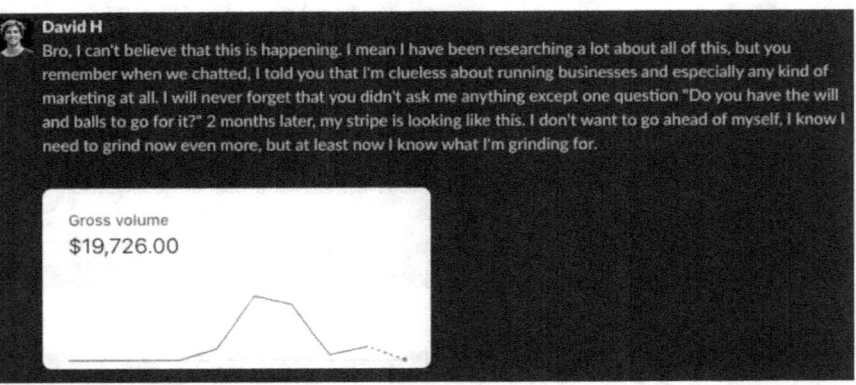

Klaus G

Finally, we passed the 10.000 euro mark, first 10k+ months are coming lightning fast! God bless the last email template, it's a killer! 🚀🚀

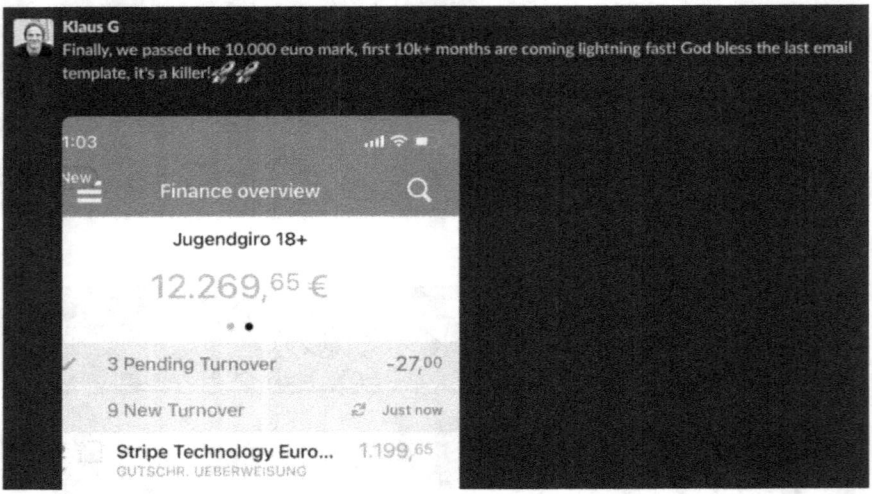

Vishu D

Third deal this month. Paid in 2 settlements.
I have 0 trouble selling the offer; it's ridiculous that even without sales skills, I'm selling $1000+ services.
Guys, It's all about offers; listen, Fran.
I paid my team immediately and pocketed the difference.

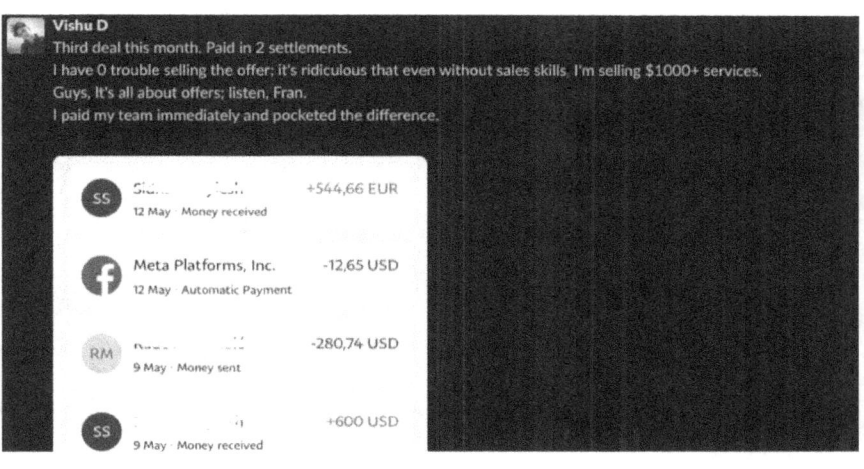

Marcus P
November
New clients: 2
Existing: 4

The $2500 a month offer works like a charm + percentages we gonna take. I think this is the winner

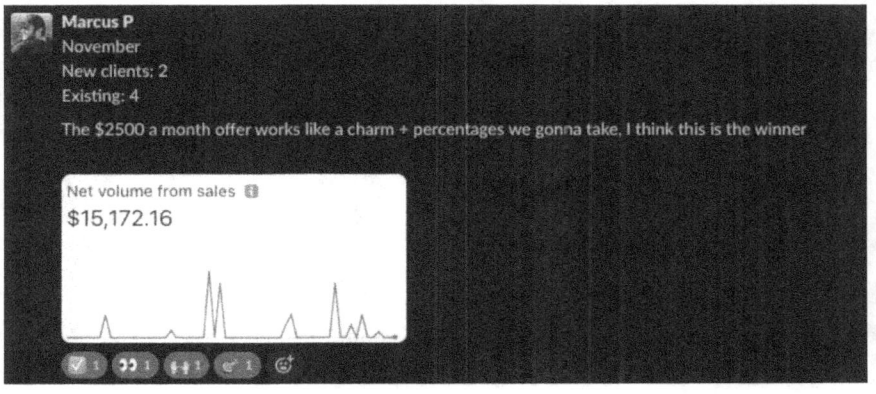

Julius I

Community, welcome to my new crib! $2k/m, paid by one of my lovely clients 😂

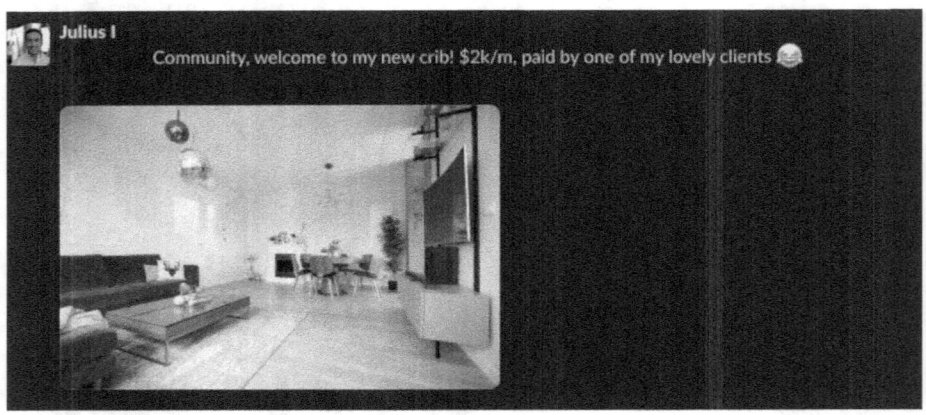

Han Y

I have been quiet for some time, but I'll let the comments now make the noise 🚀
My first car ever, my dream car.

Peter K
Almost our first $10k DAY! NOT MONTH, DAY! We had 3 follow-up calls today and all 3 of them were closed haha, the feeling after the last follow-up call was something I can't describe, I felt like Jordan Belfort on steroids 😂😂

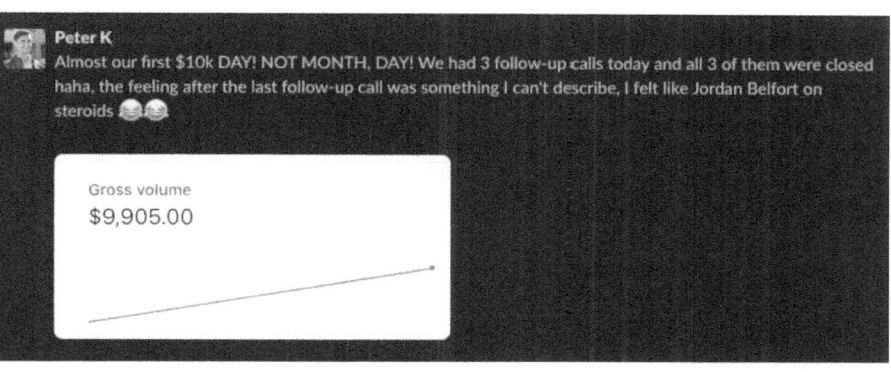

Mark J:
Another one today but the fifth this month! Small $1,500 retainer, e-com! Guys, This is changing my life for real

Marcelo P

Today we crossed $50.000 per month. $51.500 to be precise. We still have 6 days left till the end of this month and 4 more appointments booked. It took us exactly 4 months to hit this milestone, but it's the first of many, Thanks Fran for the guidance and support, this will not be possible without you. The rest of the love I'm sending to this wonderful community, I can't describe how much I'm grateful for all the support.

Klaus H

Marcus sent Stripe ss yesterday, so I need to send one as well to show the German power 😄😂

This is from 3 clients, retainer + performance, they said they plan to sign a 3-year contract.

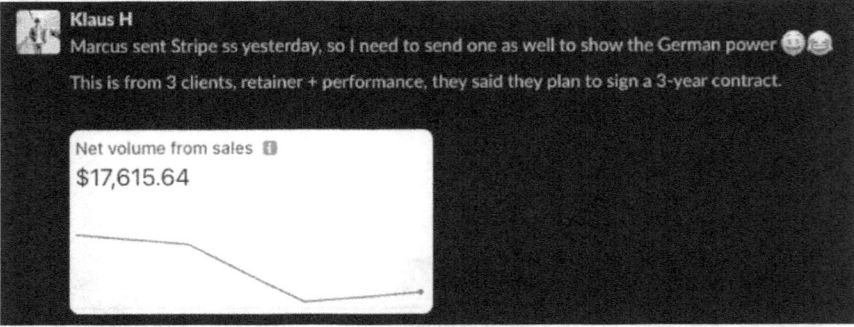

Net volume from sales

$17,615.64

Hubertus W
Yessir! January looking bright!
I know the community is signing bigger checks, but as a beginner, I'm happy that this is slowly replacing my 9-5.
Can anyone help me with the agreement? Need to send it.

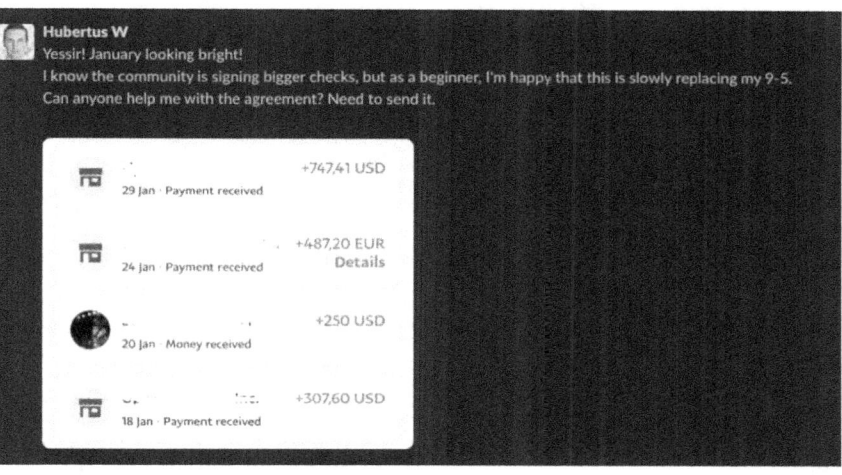

Josip R
I thought Health Lead Gen would be hard as I don't have any experience with Social Media Marketing, but I trusted Fran's expertise.
1 Month in, we have our first client.
I only charged the small retainer, tbh I got scared on call but we arranged 20% of every appointment would go to us.
Fingers crossed! Thank you everyone for your support!

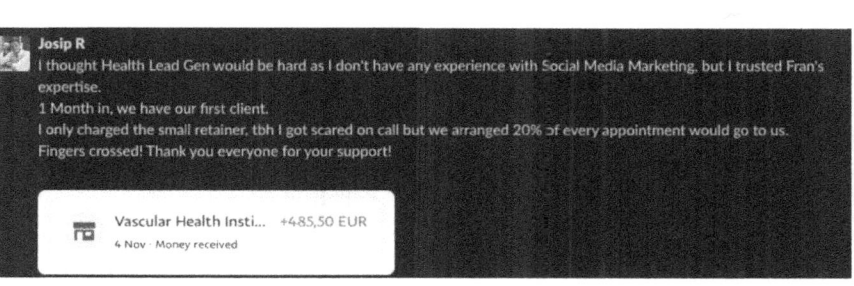

Marcel U
So close....
October was almost our first $10k/m.
But I cant be ungrateful, 7 months ago I was working for $700 a month.
I'm confident that in November we will hit more than $10k, our client retention is insane.
All the clients I signed 5 months ago are still with us, satisfied and happy. (edited)

Ante S
Hey guys, I just want to say that this was the best investment of my life, so happy to be here surrounded by like-minded people that genuinely want to help you.
You guys do not even realize that I get more support from this community than from my own friends and family.
I can't wait to meet all of you on in person.
Let's go Booois!

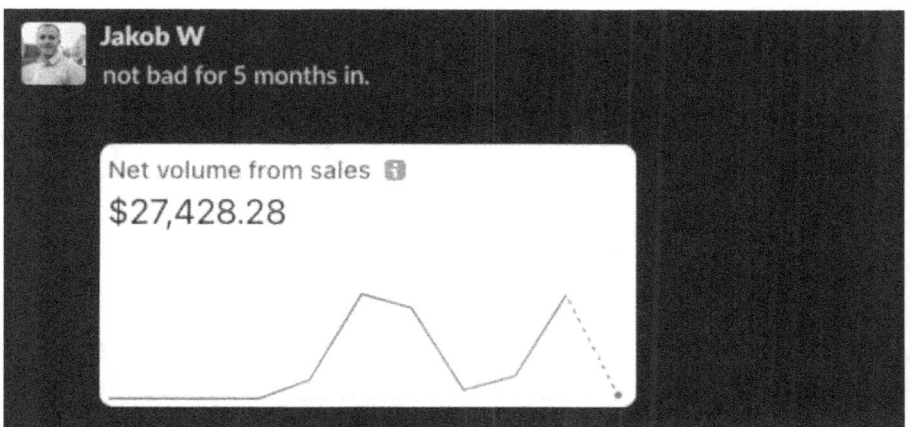

Emanuel B
Drake ~ Flight Booked playing slowly in the background 👀
4 Clients
2 Months in
Where are we flying next Community? 😄

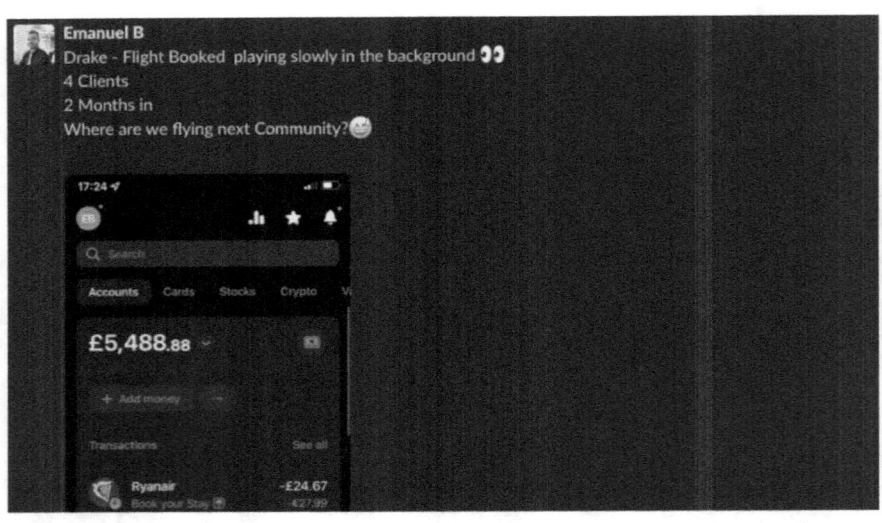

Jack M
New Client doesn't look bad at all.
After a month and a half finally we landed a big fish.
$30k/m in ad spend.
$2500 retainer + 10% performance fee.
Any tips boys?

You owe it to a 14 year old self.